# Making Twelve

Colleen Jones

Toronto

The children begin to make party bags.

"We need twelve tops,
and there are six in each pack.
How many packs did we buy?
Tell me, Jack!"

"With six in each pack,
we bought two packs," said Jack.

"We need twelve horns, and there are four in each pack. How many packs did we buy? Tell me, Jack!"

"With four in each pack,
we bought three packs," said Jack.

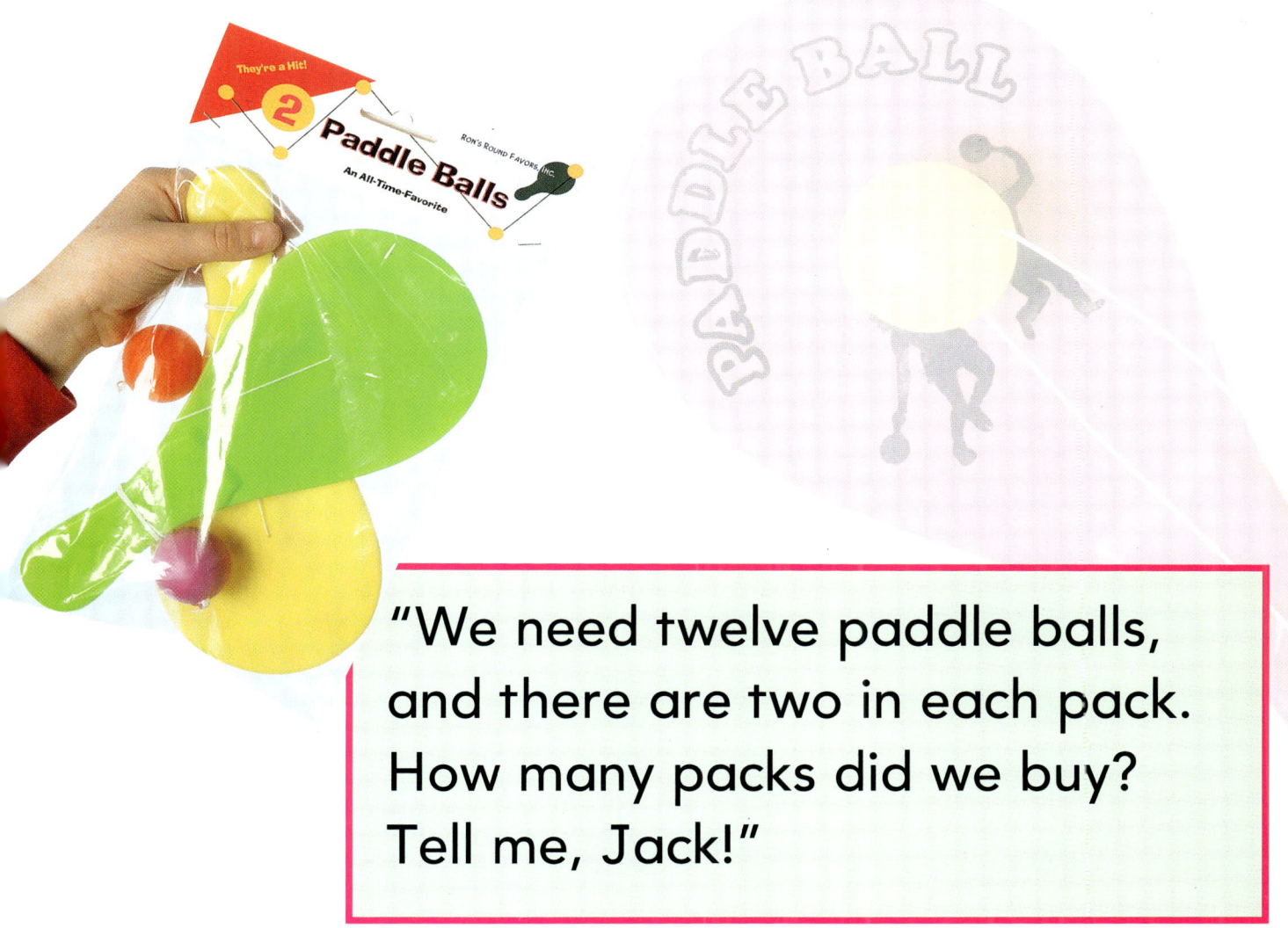

"We need twelve paddle balls, and there are two in each pack. How many packs did we buy? Tell me, Jack!"

"With two in each pack,
we bought six packs," said Jack.

"We need twelve yo-yos,
and there are three in each pack.
How many packs did we buy?
Tell me, Jack!"

"With three in each pack,
we bought four packs," said Jack.

"We need twelve party noisemakers, and there are eight in each pack. How many packs did we buy? Tell me, Jack!"

"With eight in each pack,
we bought two packs," said Jack.
"And we'll have some left over
for the next time."

"We need twelve balloons,
and there are twelve in each pack.
How many packs did we buy?
Tell me, Jack!"

"With twelve in each pack,
we bought one pack," said Jack.

"There are twelve kids altogether. We have twelve party bags."

"We took the toys from every pack. What fun we'll have!" said Jack.